What's Inside Me?
My Bones and Muscles

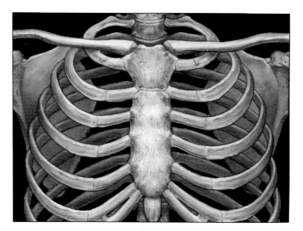

Dana Meachen Rau

BENCHMARK BOOKS

MARSHALL CAVENDISH
NEW YORK

My Bones

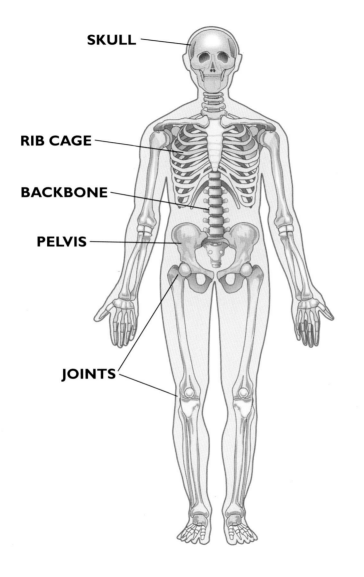

SKULL

RIB CAGE

BACKBONE

PELVIS

JOINTS

Stand still. Bend over. Wave
your arms. Kick your legs.

Your bones and your muscles help your body do all of these things.

Have you ever seen a house being built? First, it needs a *framework*. This keeps the house standing.

Your bones are the framework for your body. Without bones, your skin and inside parts would fall to the floor.

You have 206 bones in your body. All your bones together are called your *skeleton*.

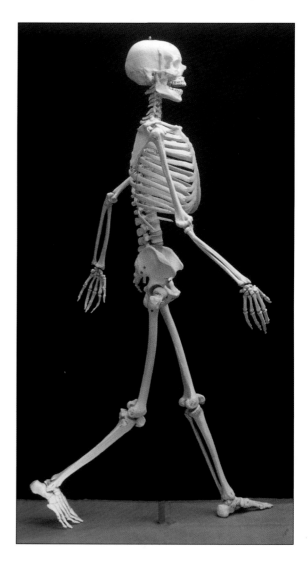

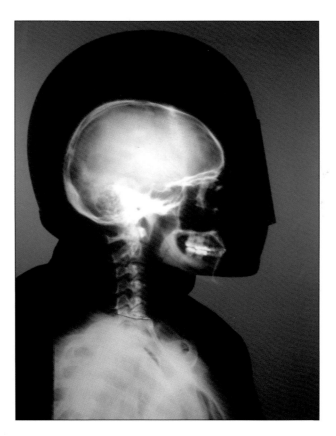

You can see your skeleton with an *X-ray*.

Look closely at a bone. The outside is hard. The inside is soft and filled with tiny holes.

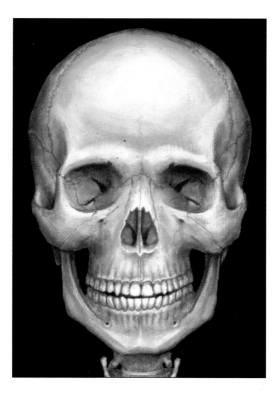

Your *skull* is made up of many flat bones. Your skull protects your brain.

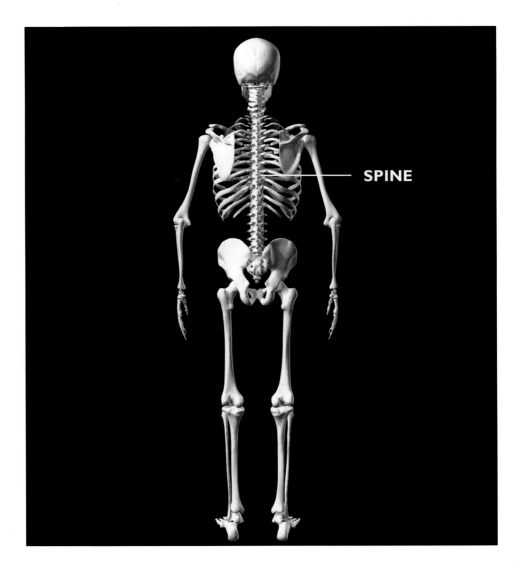

SPINE

The small round bones down your back make up your *spine*. Your spine helps you stand straight.

You have long bones in your arms and legs. You have tiny bones in your hands and feet.

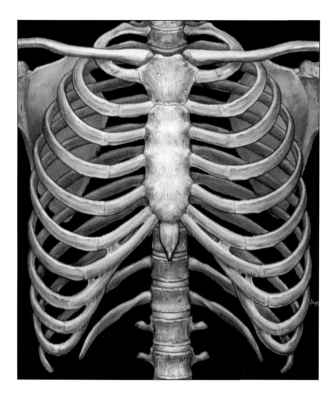

Your *rib cage* is made up of the curved bones in your chest. It protects your heart and lungs.

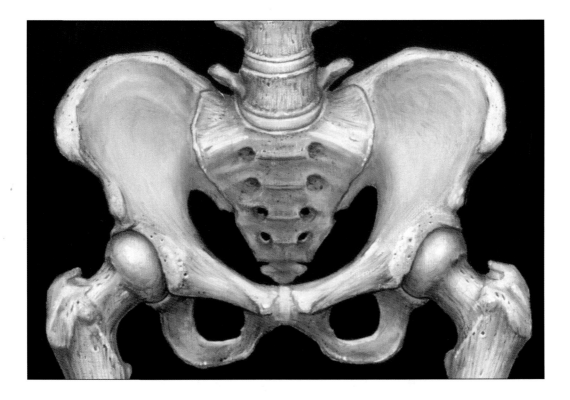

Your *pelvis* is a large, flat bone.
It helps hold up your body.

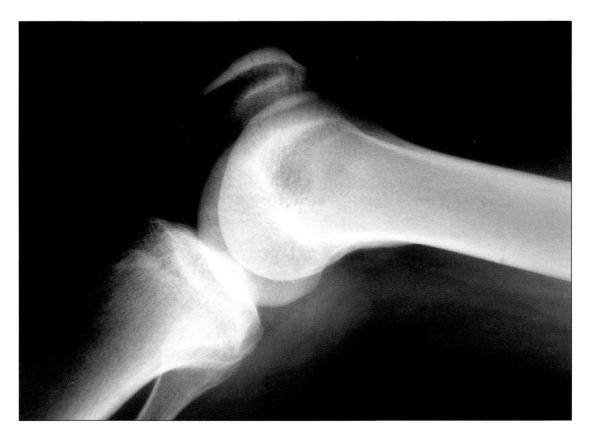

X-ray of a knee joint

A *joint* is where two bones meet. *Ligaments* connect these bones to each other.

Joints in your elbows and knees move in one direction. Joints in your shoulders and wrists move around in a circle.

Bones cannot move without muscles. Most muscles are red and striped.

There are more than 600 muscles in your body.

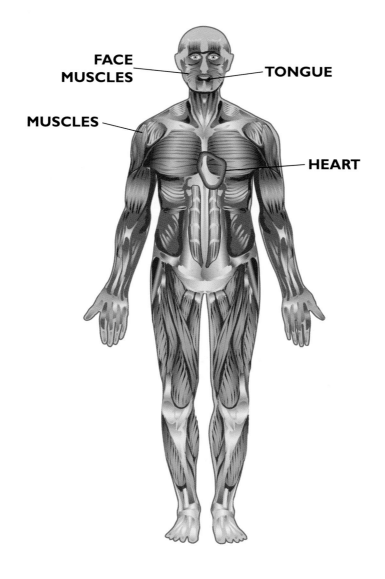

FACE MUSCLES

TONGUE

MUSCLES

HEART

19

Your hand muscles help you write a letter. You use your leg and foot muscles when you walk or run.

Every time you move, your muscles are at work.

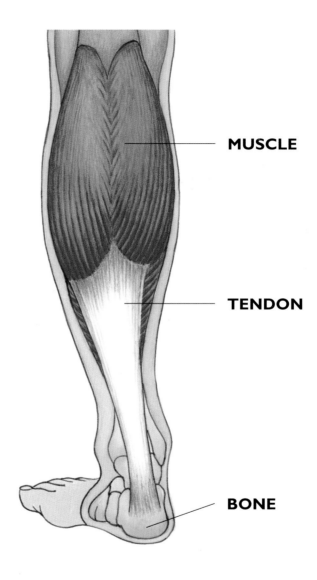

MUSCLE

TENDON

BONE

22

Strong cords called *tendons* attach muscles to bones. When a muscle moves, it pulls the bone.

That is how you can raise your hand or point with your finger.

Muscles in your face move your eyebrows, mouth, and cheeks to make you look sad, happy, or angry. You use about 17 face muscles when you smile.

Some muscles have other jobs, too. Your tongue is a muscle. It helps you swallow food.

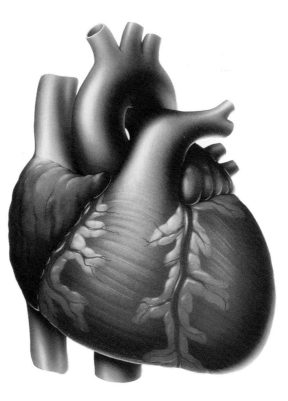

Your heart is a muscle. It pumps
blood around your body.

Your body needs exercise. Get out of your chair and take a walk with a friend. It will keep your bones and muscles strong.

Challenge Words

framework—The stiff inside parts that keep something standing up.

joint—Where two bones meet.

ligaments—Bands of body tissue that connect one bone to another.

pelvis—A large, flat bone in your hips.

rib cage—The curved bones in your chest.

skeleton (SKEL-i-tuhn)—All of your bones.

skull—The bones in your head.

spine—The line of small bones running down your back.

tendons (TEN-duhns)—Strong cords that attach muscles to bones.

X-ray—A picture of your bones.

Index

Page numbers in **boldface** are illustrations.

With thanks to Nanci Vargus, Ed.D.
and Beth Walker Gambro, reading consultants

Benchmark Books
Marshall Cavendish
99 White Plains Road
Tarrytown, New York 10591-9001
www.marshallcavendish.com

Library of Congress Cataloging-in-Publication Data

Rau, Dana Meachen, 1971–
My bones and muscles / by Dana Meachen Rau.
p. cm. — (Bookworms: What's inside me?)
Includes index.
ISBN 0-7614-1777-X
1. Musculoskeletal system—Juvenile literature. I. Title. II. Series.

QM100.R38 2004
612.7—dc22
2004006386

Photo Research by Anne Burns Images

Cover Photo by *Corbis*/Royalty Free

The photographs in this book are published with the permission and through the courtesy of:
Peter Arnold: pp. 1, 11, 14, 15 Alex Grey; p. 8 Manfred Kage; p. 9 James V. Elmore; pp. 10, 16 Ed Reschke.
Jay Mallin: p. 2. *Corbis*: p. 5 Franco Vogt; p. 6 Joseph Sohm; pp. 4, 20 LWA-Dann Tardif; p. 21 Norbert Schaefer;
p. 25 Tom & Dee Ann McCarthy; pp. 26 Torleif Svensson; p. 28 Royalty Free.
Photo Researchers: p. 12 Roger Harris; p. 27 Brian Evans. *Custom Medical Stock Photo*: p. 22.

Series design by Becky Terhune
Illustrations by Ian Warpole

Printed in China
1 3 5 6 4 2